IT'S YOUR TIME TO SHINE

Sura Khan

Design by: VSE Enterprises LLC

Library of Congress Cataloging – in-Publication Data

ISBN: 9798864762165

Table of Contents

2 Corinthians 6:2

For he says, "In a favorable **time** I listened to you, and in a day of salvation I have helped you." Behold, now is the favorable **time**; behold, now is the day of salvation.

THE WORD

The Power is in the Word!
A Word contains three important essentials, Energy,
Light and Power.
The Power of your belief in the Word cracks it open
and all that is bound in the word is now unleashed
you.

Introduction

These writings are for all those seeking their place in this world. Those who know that they are here for a purpose. Those who know deep within that they have a job to fulfill but don't know the big question. What is the big question? The Time. When is the time for me, you ask yourself? I'm here to tell you that the time is Now! Now is your time to shine.

Some cannot imagine a world without the cell phone Internet, or social media. There was a time when none of these things existed. The vision for these things was sitting inside an individual; Steve Jobs is one of them. He saw that the world could be a different place with the computer and decided to take action. It's challenging to bring something out of nothing or make something altogether new or do something that has never been done before. It all starts with a thought and a desire to see something different that can change how the world moves. Like growing a child in its mother's womb, there must be a period when all the pieces come together in that dark place. A place that was not visible to the human eye at a time. Bringing your vision to light is something like that. No one can see what is happening in the process of your creation. You are alone. There's no one to cheer you on. Just that spark of something deep within yourself pushes you to bring something forth. In time, this creation will be your reality if it's not aborted.

The biggest obstacle in our way is nine times out of ten ourselves. We try to believe in ourselves when no one else does—allowing distractions to stop our process, working hard when no one can see what we are doing or thinking, and trying to manage our day-to-day life, family, and other essential factors while bringing our vision to life. These are not simple things to do, but it has been done repeatedly. These visionaries are no different than you and me. We all have the same capacity, brains, and minds to create. One of the critical components is to not worry about how you will do it and think more about what you will do. Leave the money you need and the other resources you require to time and faith. It will all be there for you when you need it. That's faith, the big part.

My question for you is, what will you do or bring to the world that can help others and advance yourself, your family, and your community in the process? Is it Art, Music, Writing, Food, Ministry, or Medicine? What is it, do you know? This book is in your presence at this moment in time as a guild, motivation, and inspiration to move you closer to that space in time where you can truly shine.

I have double-spaced the text so that you can add notes under various sentences if you wish. You will also notice that some sentences are repeated in different ways in other chapters, repeatedly. I did this purposefully so that the sub-conscience mind wouldn't miss the word's importance and power. Now let's journey on.

Dedication

To my Children, Lyrics Leon, Twanda Parris and

Dondre. My Grandchildren, Great-Grand Children,

Siblings and Family. Apostle Linda Weaver. Thank

you for sharing me with the world so that I might

help us all find our place in time and shine.

Acknowledgments

Special thank you to all those who helped me to

shine thus far throughout this wonderful journey

called life. Not enough space to mention everyone..

Divine A Kirkman, Henry Koon, Will Carter, Bobby

Bostick, Kenney Sattaur, Terri Patterson, among many

others.

It's Your Time to Shine

"The Balance Between Spirituality & Creativity"

CHAPTER ONE

It's Your Time To Shine: Harnessing Your Inner Motivation & Understanding Spirituality

It's your time to shine. This is the moment you've been waiting for, the moment when you can harness the power of your inner motivation and truly shine. Motivation, that inner drive that pushes us to achieve our goals and overcome obstacles, is the key to unlocking our full potential. It is the fuel that propels us forward, even when faced with challenges and setbacks. But how do we tap into this powerful force within us? The first step is to recognize that motivation comes from within. It is not something that can be given to us or forced upon us. It is a flame that burns deep within our souls, waiting to be ignited. To harness your inner motivation, you must first understand what truly drives you. What are your passions? What are your dreams? Take a moment to reflect on these questions and truly listen to your heart's desires. Once you have identified your true motivations, it's time to set goals that align with them. These goals should be specific, measurable, attainable, relevant, and time-bound. By setting clear objectives, you give yourself a roadmap to success and a sense of direction. But setting goals is just the beginning. The next step is to develop a plan of action. Break down your goals into smaller, manageable steps and create a timeline for each one. This will help you stay focused and organized as you work towards your ultimate objective. However, simply having a plan is not enough. It's important to stay committed and disciplined along the way. There will be days when you feel tired or discouraged, but it is during these times that your inner motivation will shine the brightest. Remind yourself of why you started this journey in the first place and draw strength from the fire within. Surrounding yourself with a supportive network is also crucial. Seek out like-minded individuals who share your goals and aspirations. Their positive energy and encouragement will fuel your motivation and propel you forward. Don't be afraid to ask for help when you need it, as collaboration and support can make all the difference. As you progress towards your goals, take the time to celebrate your achievements, no matter how small they may seem. Each step forward is a step closer to realizing your full potential and shining brightly. Remember, it's your time to shine. Harness the power of your inner motivation and let it guide you towards greatness. Believe in yourself, stay focused, and never give up. With determination and perseverance, you will reach new heights and inspire others to do the same. Now is the time to embrace your inner fire and let it illuminate the path ahead. It's your time to shine.

Understanding Spirituality In the vast tapestry of human experience, there exists a realm that transcends the boundaries of our physical existence. It is a realm that speaks to the deepest parts of our being, offering solace, guidance, and a profound sense of connection. This realm is spirituality. Spirituality is a concept that has been explored, debated, and embraced by cultures throughout history. It is a deeply personal and subjective experience, unique to each individual. Yet, despite its diversity, spirituality shares a common thread that weaves through the fabric of human existence – a search for meaning, purpose, and a connection to something greater than ourselves. To understand spirituality is to embark on a journey of self-discovery and exploration. It is a journey that requires an open mind, a receptive heart, and a willingness to delve into the depths of our inner being. It is a journey that transcends the boundaries of religion, dogma, and tradition, for spirituality is not confined to any specific belief system. It is a universal language that speaks to the essence of our humanity.

At its core, spirituality is about cultivating a sense of connection – a connection to ourselves, to others, to the natural world, and to the divine. It is about recognizing that we are part of something greater, something that transcends the limitations of our physical existence. It is about awakening to the profound interconnectedness of all things and embracing the inherent wisdom and beauty that permeates the universe. Understanding spirituality requires us to tap into our innermost depths, to quiet the noise of the external world, and to listen to the whispers of our soul. It is a journey of self-reflection, introspection, and contemplation. It is about uncovering our true essence, our authentic self, and aligning our thoughts, words, and actions with this inner truth. Spirituality is not limited to the realm of the ethereal; it is also intimately intertwined with our creative expression. Creativity is a powerful force that flows through us, allowing us to tap into our innate potential and bring forth something new into the world. When we merge spirituality and creativity, we create a harmonious dance, a dance that allows us to channel divine inspiration and infuse our creations with depth, meaning, and purpose. To understand spirituality is to embrace the interconnectedness of all things, to recognize the divine spark within ourselves and others, and to cultivate a sense of wonder, awe, and reverence for the world around us. It is a journey that calls us to live authentically, to embody our highest values, and to engage in a lifelong quest for growth, transformation, and enlightenment. May this understanding of spirituality guide you on your path, illuminating the way and inspiring you to embrace the fullness of your being. May it empower you to unleash your creative potential, to manifest your dreams, and to contribute to the world in a way that aligns with your deepest values and aspirations. Remember, dear reader, that spirituality is not a destination but a journey. It is a journey of self-discovery, connection, and transformation. Embrace it wholeheartedly, for in doing so, you will unlock the secrets of the universe and discover the true essence of your soul.

CHAPTER TWO

Uncovering Your True Potential & Understanding Creativity

Welcome to a journey of self-discovery and personal growth. As you turn the pages of this book, you will embark on a path that leads you to unlock the hidden potential within you. It's a journey that requires dedication, perseverance, and a belief in your own limitless capabilities. We live in a world that often places limits on what we can achieve. Society tells us what is possible and what is not, leading many to settle for a life that is far below their true potential. But deep within each of us lies the power to defy these limitations and create a life that is extraordinary. Uncovering your true potential is about shedding the layers of doubt, fear, and self-imposed limitations that have held you back. It's about stepping into the light and embracing the unique gifts and talents that make you who you are. It's about realizing that you are capable of achieving greatness in any area of your life. But how do we uncover this potential? How do we tap into the wellspring of greatness that lies within us? The first step is to believe. Believe in yourself, in your dreams, and in your ability to turn those dreams into reality. Believe that you are deserving of success, happiness, and fulfillment. Believe that you have what it takes to overcome any obstacle and achieve your goals. Next, it's important to set clear and meaningful goals. Take the time to reflect on what truly matters to you and what you want to achieve in life. Write down your goals and create a plan of action to bring them to fruition. Break them down into smaller, manageable steps, and celebrate each milestone along the way. As you embark on this journey of self-discovery, it's crucial to cultivate a positive mindset. Surround yourself with positive influences and inspirational role models. Seek out opportunities for personal growth and self-improvement. Embrace challenges as opportunities for growth, and learn from your failures as stepping stones to success. Self-reflection is another powerful tool in uncovering your true potential. Take the time to understand your strengths, weaknesses, and areas for growth. Be honest with yourself about your passions, values, and aspirations. By gaining a deeper understanding of who you are, you can align your actions and choices with your authentic self. Remember, uncovering your true potential is not a destination but a lifelong journey. It requires continuous effort, self-reflection, and an unwavering belief in your ability to create the life you desire. Embrace the challenges, celebrate your successes, and never stop striving for greatness. As you move forward on this path, remember that you are capable of far more than you can ever imagine. Embrace the journey of uncovering your true potential and watch as your life transforms in extraordinary ways. It's your time to shine, so go forth and unleash the boundless potential within you.

Understanding Creativity   In the realm of human existence, there exists a fascinating interplay between spirituality and creativity. Both are deeply intertwined, feeding off each other's energy and nourishing the depths of the human soul. To truly grasp the essence of creativity, one must embark on a journey of understanding. Creativity, at its core, is a spiritual force that arises from the depths of the human spirit. It is a divine spark that ignites our imagination, enabling us to bring forth new ideas, innovation, and beauty into the world. When we tap into our creative potential, we are connecting with a higher power, accessing a universal flow of inspiration and insight. To understand creativity is to recognize its inherent connection to spirituality. It is the inner and outer worlds, a harmonious symphony of the mind, body, and soul. When we engage in creative endeavors, we are not merely producing art or expressing ourselves; we are attuning ourselves to the divine energy that permeates all existence. Creativity is not limited to the realm of traditional artistic pursuits. It is a force that extends beyond the boundaries of any specific medium or discipline. It manifests in various forms, whether it be through the strokes of a painter's brush, the melodies of a musician's composition, the words on a writer's page, or even the innovative ideas of an entrepreneur. Creativity is the life force that breathes vitality into all aspects of human expression. To truly understand creativity, one must embrace the inherent connection between spirituality and the creative process. It is in the depths of our spiritual being that we find the wellspring of inspiration, the source of our creative power. By cultivating a deeper connection with our spirituality, we open ourselves to the infinite possibilities that creativity holds. Spirituality provides the foundation upon which creativity can bloom. It offers us a sense of purpose, a connection to something greater than ourselves. When we align ourselves with our spiritual essence, we tap into a well of wisdom and intuition that guides our creative endeavors. It is through this alignment that we can fully express our unique talents and gifts, infusing our creations with authenticity and depth. In understanding creativity, we must also recognize the importance of balance. Just as spirituality nourishes creativity, creativity, in turn, nourishes spirituality. The act of creation itself is a spiritual practice, a means of connecting with the divine. It allows us to transcend the limits of the material world and touch the eternal essence that resides within us all. To find balance between spirituality and creativity is to embrace the interconnectedness of these two profound aspects of our human experience. It is to recognize that they are not separate entities but rather threads woven together in the tapestry of our existence. By nurturing both our spirituality and our creativity, we can embark on a transformative journey of self-discovery and self-expression. In this chapter, we have delved into the depths of creativity, exploring its intrinsic link to spirituality. We have come to understand that creativity is not simply a product of our minds but a manifestation of our souls. It is a gateway to the divine, a channel through which we can access the infinite wellspring of inspiration that resides within us. By embracing the balance between spirituality and creativity, we can unlock the full potential of our creative beings and embark on a path of profound growth and fulfillment.

CHAPTER THREE

Breaking Through Self-Imposed Limitations & Finding the Balance in Spirituality and Creativity

Welcome, dear reader, to the transformative journey of breaking through self-imposed limitations. In this chapter, we will delve deep into the power of overcoming the barriers we create within ourselves, and how it can lead us to shine brightly in our lives. Each one of us possesses immense potential, yet oftentimes we find ourselves held back by our own doubts, fears, and negative beliefs. These self-imposed limitations can act as invisible chains, preventing us from reaching our true potential and living a life of fulfillment and happiness. But fear not, for within you lies the power to break through these barriers. It's time to unleash your inner strength, embrace your true self, and let go of the limitations that have been holding you back. The first step towards breaking through self-imposed limitations is to recognize and acknowledge them. Take a moment to reflect on your life and identify areas where you have been holding yourself back. Are there certain dreams and aspirations that you have dismissed as impossible? Have you constantly doubted your abilities or settled for less than what you truly desire? Once you have identified these limitations, it's essential to challenge them head-on. Understand that these limitations are merely perceptions, not absolute truths. They are products of past experiences, societal conditioning, and perhaps even the opinions of others. But they do not define who you are or what you are capable of achieving. Now, it's time to reframe your mindset. Take a moment to imagine a life without these self-imposed limitations. How would you feel? What goals would you pursue? Visualize yourself living a life where you are free from the shackles of doubt and fear. Allow yourself to believe that you are deserving of success, happiness, and fulfillment. Breaking through self-imposed limitations requires a commitment to personal growth and a willingness to step outside of your comfort zone. It may not always be easy, but remember that growth happens outside of our comfort zones. Embrace the discomfort and trust that you are capable of navigating through any challenges that come your way. Surround yourself with a support system that uplifts and encourages you. Seek out mentors, friends, or like-minded individuals who have already broken through their own limitations. Their stories and guidance can provide you with inspiration and practical strategies to overcome your own barriers. Lastly, practice self-compassion throughout this journey. Understand that breaking through self-imposed limitations is a process that takes time and effort. Be patient with yourself and celebrate every small victory along the way. Remember, you are on a path towards personal growth and self-discovery, and each step forward is a step closer to shining brightly in your life. Now, dear reader, it's time to embark on this empowering journey of breaking through self-imposed limitations. Embrace your true potential, challenge your beliefs, and let go of the limitations that have been holding you back. It's your time to shine, and the world eagerly awaits your brilliance.

Finding the Balance in Spirituality & Creativity In the realm of human existence, there are two profound forces that shape our lives: spirituality and creativity. These forces have the power to fuel our passions, drive our actions, and bring meaning to our journey. However, it is often a delicate situation to find the balance between these two essential aspects of our being. Spirituality is the connection to something greater than ourselves, a transcendent force that guides us on a deeper level. It is the wellspring of our beliefs, the source of our values, and the compass that helps us navigate the complexities of life. Spirituality provides us with a sense of purpose, a grounding in the present moment, and a connection to the divine. On the other hand, creativity is the spark that ignites our imagination and allows us to express ourselves authentically. It is the gateway to our inner world, where ideas flow freely and possibilities abound. Creativity is the driving force behind innovation, art, and the exploration of new horizons. It is the vessel through which we can communicate our deepest emotions and connect with others on a profound level. Yet, in our pursuit of spirituality and creativity, it is easy to become imbalanced. We may find ourselves too focused on the ethereal realms, neglecting our earthly responsibilities and passions.

Alternatively, we may become so consumed by our creative endeavors that we lose sight of our spiritual essence, disconnected from the deeper meaning of our actions. So how can we find the delicate balance between spirituality and creativity? How can we cultivate a harmonious relationship between these two powerful forces within us? The first step is to recognize that spirituality and creativity are not mutually exclusive, but rather intertwined aspects of our being. They complement and nourish each other, like two sides of the same coin. When we engage in creative pursuits with a sense of spirituality, we infuse our creations with depth and meaning. Likewise, when we approach our spirituality with a creative mindset, we open ourselves to new insights and experiences. To find balance, we must cultivate mindfulness in both our spiritual and creative practices. By being fully present in the moment, we can honor the divine essence within us and tap into our creative potential. Through meditation, prayer, or contemplation, we can quiet the mind, connect with our inner selves, and invite inspiration to flow. Similarly, we must embrace creativity as a spiritual practice. By infusing our creative endeavors with intention and awareness, we can create art that transcends the superficial and touches the soul. Engaging in creative rituals, such as journaling, painting, or dancing, can become sacred acts of self-expression and connection to the divine. It is important to remember that finding balance is an ongoing process, a continual exploration of the self. As we navigate the complexities of life, we may sway between spirituality and creativity, finding ourselves out of alignment at times. Yet, with awareness and commitment, we can always come back to center, finding our way back to the delicate balance between these two profound forces. In the journey of finding the balance in spirituality and creativity, we discover that they are not opposing forces, but rather complementary aspects of our humanity. By embracing both spirituality and creativity, we can lead a purposeful and fulfilling life, where our actions are guided by our deepest values and our creations are infused with meaning. So let us embark on this journey together, seeking the balance that lies at the intersection of spirituality and creativity. Let us embrace the divine spark within us and unleash our creative potential. In doing so, we will find a harmony that brings joy, fulfillment, and a deeper connection to ourselves and the world around us.

CHAPTER FOUR

Developing a Positive Mindset & Believing in Yourself

This chapter is where we dive deep into the power of developing a positive mindset. Within these pages, you will uncover the necessary tools and techniques to shape your thoughts, beliefs, and perspective towards a more optimistic outlook on life. It is said that the mind is like a garden; what you plant, nourish, and cultivate will eventually grow. If we constantly sow seeds of negativity, doubt, and self-limiting beliefs, that is precisely what will flourish within our minds. On the other hand, if we choose to plant seeds of positivity, hope, and self-belief, we will witness the beauty of a bountiful and prosperous mental garden. Developing a positive mindset is not about denying the existence of challenges or pretending that life is always a bed of roses. It is about consciously choosing to focus on the good, the possibilities, and the lessons that each experience presents. It is about recognizing that setbacks and obstacles are merely detours on the road to success, rather than dead ends. One of the fundamental aspects of developing a positive mindset is the practice of gratitude. Gratitude opens our eyes to the abundance that already exists in our lives. By shifting our focus from what we lack to what we have, we invite more blessings and opportunities into our path. Take a moment each day to express gratitude for the simple joys, the supportive relationships, and the lessons learned from adversity. As you cultivate an attitude of gratitude, you will notice a profound shift in your mindset. Another powerful tool in developing a positive mindset is affirmations. Affirmations are positive statements that you repeat to yourself to rewire your subconscious mind. By consistently affirming your desired beliefs and goals, you begin to reshape your thoughts and reprogram your mind for success. Create affirmations that reflect the mindset you wish to embody, such as "I am deserving of all the good that comes into my life" or "I have the power to overcome any challenge." Repeat these affirmations daily, with conviction and belief, to reinforce a positive mindset. In addition to gratitude and affirmations, surrounding yourself with positive influences is crucial. Be mindful of the company you keep, as the people you spend time with have a significant impact on your mindset. Surround yourself with individuals who uplift, support, and inspire you. Seek out mentors, role models, and positive communities that align with your goals and values. Their positivity and encouragement will fuel your motivation and reinforce your positive mindset. Finally, self-care plays a vital role in developing a positive mindset. Nurturing your mind, body, and soul allows you to operate at your highest potential. Prioritize activities that bring you joy, peace, and fulfillment. Engage in regular exercise, practice mindfulness or meditation, indulge in hobbies, and make time for rest and relaxation. By taking care of yourself holistically, you create a solid foundation for positivity and resilience. Remember, developing a positive mindset is not an overnight process. It requires consistent effort, self-awareness, and a commitment to personal growth. Embrace the journey, and celebrate the small victories along the way. As you continue to cultivate a positive mindset, you will attract abundance, overcome obstacles, and shine brightly in all areas of your life. In conclusion, developing a positive mindset is a transformative journey that begins with your thoughts, beliefs, and perspective. By consciously choosing optimism, practicing gratitude, affirming your desires, surrounding yourself with positivity, and prioritizing self-care, you unlock the incredible power within you. It's your time to shine, and with a positive mindset, the possibilities are limitless.

Believing in Yourself. In this section, we will explore an essential aspect of the delicate moves between spirituality and creativity: the unwavering belief in oneself. It is through this unwavering belief that we can unleash our true potential and tap into the vast well of inspiration that lies within. Believing in yourself is not a mere act of wishful thinking or blind optimism. It is a deep-rooted conviction that stems from a profound understanding of your own worth and capabilities. When you have faith in yourself, you become unstoppable, capable of transcending limitations and pushing the boundaries of your creativity. To truly believe in oneself, one must first cultivate a genuine sense of self-awareness. This involves taking the time to reflect on your strengths, weaknesses, and unique qualities. It is through this self-discovery that you will come to appreciate your own inherent worth and recognize the immense potential that resides within you. However, believing in oneself also requires a willingness to embrace vulnerability. It is in those moments of doubt and uncertainty that our belief in ourselves is truly tested. It is during these times that we must summon the courage to confront our fears and push through the discomfort. It is through these challenges that we grow and evolve, forging an even deeper belief in our abilities. Seek out individuals who uplift and inspire you, who recognize and celebrate your unique gifts. Their unwavering belief in you will serve as a constant reminder of your own potential, reinforcing the belief you have in yourself. Each small step forward is a testament to your belief in yourself and a validation of your abilities. Take the time to honor your progress, no matter how small it may seem. By doing so, you will fuel your belief in yourself and propel yourself even further on your creative journey. Finally, remember that belief in oneself is an ongoing practice. It requires daily commitment and conscious effort. There will be moments when self-doubt creeps in, but it is in those moments that you must remind yourself of your worth and reaffirm your belief in your own abilities. Believing in yourself is not always easy, but it is an essential ingredient in the balance between spirituality and creativity. It is through this belief that we find ourselves, allowing time to guide and inspire our creative endeavors. I urge you to embrace your worth, cultivate self-belief, and watch as the magic of your creativity unfolds before your very eyes.

CHAPTER FIVE

Overcoming Fear and Anxiety & Believing In Your Vision

Overcoming Fear and Anxiety is a transformative journey towards shining your brightest. In the previous chapters, we have explored various aspects of self-discovery, personal growth, and the pursuit of our dreams. Now, it is time to confront the formidable barriers that hinder our progress and rob us of our shine: fear and anxiety. Fear and anxiety are two powerful emotions that can hold us back from achieving our true potential. They have the ability to cloud our judgment, paralyze our actions, and prevent us from stepping into the spotlight of our lives. But fear not, for within you lies the strength to overcome these obstacles and embrace the brilliance that is waiting to burst forth. To begin, let us understand fear and anxiety for what they truly are – mere illusions, created by our minds. They are the stories we tell ourselves, the limitations we impose upon ourselves, and the walls we build around ourselves. But just as we have the power to create these illusions, we also possess the power to dismantle them. The first step in overcoming fear and anxiety is to acknowledge their presence. We must become aware of the thoughts and emotions that arise when faced with challenging situations. Take a moment to observe how fear manifests in your body – the racing heart, the shallow breaths, the tense muscles. Recognize anxiety as the restless mind, constantly projecting worst-case scenarios, and robbing you of your peace. Once you have acknowledged fear and anxiety, it is time to face them head-on. Embrace them as opportunities for growth rather than obstacles to be avoided. Remember, the greatest achievements often lie just beyond our comfort zones. It is in these moments of discomfort that we have the chance to rise above our fears and shine brighter than ever before. To conquer fear, we must be willing to take risks. Start small, with baby steps that gradually push you beyond your perceived limitations. Each small victory will build your confidence and propel you forward towards greater triumphs. As you face your fears, remind yourself of your purpose, your passion, and the immense potential that resides within you. Let these be your guiding lights as you navigate the uncharted territories

of your shine. Anxiety, on the other hand, can be

tamed through the power of mindfulness. Practice

being fully present in the here and now, rather than

allowing your mind to wander into the realms of

worry and doubt. Engage in activities that ground

you, such as meditation, deep breathing exercises, or

journaling. Cultivate a sense of gratitude for the

present moment, recognizing that anxiety is often

born from a fixation on an uncertain future.

Remember, dear reader, that fear and anxiety are not

permanent states of being. They are merely passing

clouds in the vast sky of your life. Embrace the

discomfort, for it is in these moments that you grow,

evolve, and become the best version of yourself. As

you confront your fears and dissolve the shackles of anxiety, you will find yourself stepping into the spotlight, radiating with the brilliance that is uniquely yours. It is your time to shine, dear reader. Embrace the challenges, conquer your fears, and let your light illuminate the world. You have within you the strength, the resilience, and the unwavering spirit to overcome fear and anxiety. Believe in yourself, trust in the journey, and know that the time for you to shine is now.

Believing in Your Vision In the realm of spirituality and creativity, there lies a delicate balance that we must strive to maintain. It is faith and imagination, where our visions take flight and our souls soar. This chapter is devoted to exploring the importance of believing in your vision, for it is this belief that serves as the foundation upon which your creative endeavors can truly flourish. At the heart of every great artist, there exists a deep-seated conviction in the power of their vision. It is this unwavering belief that propels them forward, even in the face of doubt and uncertainty. When we believe in our vision, we tap into a wellspring of inspiration and motivation that can carry us through the darkest of times. But how do we cultivate this belief? How do we foster a sense of unwavering faith in our creative dreams? The journey begins with self-reflection and introspection. Take the time to question yourself: What is it that truly drives you? What is your purpose as an artist?

What is the message you wish to convey to the world? Once you have a clear understanding of your vision, it is essential to nurture it with intention and care. Seek out people who can offer valuable insights and guidance along the way. Embrace opportunities for growth and learning, as they will only serve to strengthen your belief in yourself and your vision. In the realm of spirituality, belief is a cornerstone of faith. It is the unwavering trust in something greater than ourselves, a force that guides and sustains us. Just as we believe in a higher power, we must learn to believe in the power of our own creative potential. Trust that the universe has bestowed upon you a unique vision, and it is your duty to bring it to life. As you embark on your creative journey, remember that belief is not a passive act. It requires active engagement and a willingness to take risks. It demands that you step outside of your comfort zone and confront the fear of failure head-on. Embrace the unknown and trust in the process, for it is through these challenges that we grow both as artists and as individuals. Believing in your vision also means acknowledging and embracing the inevitable setbacks and obstacles that will arise along the way. It is important to remember that failure is not a reflection of your worth or talent, but rather an opportunity for growth and refinement. Each setback is a stepping stone towards greater clarity and understanding of your vision. In the face of doubt and adversity, hold steadfast to your belief. Surround yourself with reminders of your vision, whether it be through affirmations, visualizations, or daily rituals. Allow yourself to dream big and envision the future you desire. Believe in the power of your vision to manifest itself in reality. In conclusion, believing in your vision is a fundamental aspect of the delicate balance between spirituality and creativity. It is the fuel that ignites your creative fire and propels you towards the realization of your dreams. Cultivate this belief through self-reflection, support from others, and a willingness to embrace challenges. Trust in the power of your vision and allow it to guide you on your creative journey.

CHAPTER SIX

Managing Stress and Pressure & Overcoming Challenges

Managing Stress and Pressure. In the journey towards achieving our dreams and reaching our full potential, we often encounter moments of stress and pressure. These moments can be overwhelming, causing us to doubt ourselves and our abilities. However, it is essential to understand that stress and pressure are natural parts of life. They are not meant to break us but to help us grow stronger and push ourselves beyond our limits. Managing stress and pressure is a skill that can be learned and mastered. By effectively handling these challenges, we can maintain our focus, motivation, and ultimately, shine brighter than ever before. In this chapter, we will explore various techniques and strategies that will enable us to navigate through stressful situations with grace and resilience. One of the first steps in managing stress and pressure is to recognize and acknowledge our feelings. It is crucial not to suppress or ignore them but to confront them head-on. By understanding and accepting our emotions, we can gain clarity and begin to develop a plan of action. Next, it is essential to prioritize self-care. Taking care of our physical, mental, and emotional well-being is vital in managing stress and pressure. Engaging in activities that bring us joy, practicing mindfulness and relaxation techniques, and maintaining a healthy lifestyle are all crucial aspects of self-care. By nurturing ourselves, we ensure that we have the strength and resilience to face any challenges that come our way. Furthermore, effective time management plays a significant role in managing stress and pressure. By creating a structured schedule and setting realistic goals, we can avoid becoming overwhelmed and feeling a constant sense of urgency. Breaking tasks into smaller, manageable steps allows us to allocate our time and energy efficiently, reducing stress and increasing productivity. In addition to time management, it is important to develop effective coping mechanisms. Each individual has their own unique way of handling stress, so it is essential to identify what works best for us. Some find solace in physical activities such as exercise or yoga, while others may turn to creative outlets like painting or writing. Finding healthy outlets for stress and pressure allows us to release tension and regain a sense of inner peace. Moreover, cultivating a positive mindset is crucial in managing stress and pressure. By reframing negative thoughts and focusing on the positive aspects of a situation, we can change our perspective and approach challenges with optimism. Embracing a growth mindset, where we view obstacles as opportunities for growth and learning, empowers us to overcome stress and pressure with resilience. Finally, seeking support from our loved ones or professionals can be immensely beneficial in managing stress and pressure. Opening up and sharing our concerns and fears can provide us with a fresh perspective and valuable advice. Remember, managing stress and pressure is not about eliminating them entirely, but rather, it is about developing the skills and mindset to navigate through them effectively. By implementing the strategies discussed in this chapter, you will be equipped to handle any stressful situation that arises on your journey towards shining brightly. Take a deep breath, believe in yourself, and embrace the challenges that come your way. It's your time to shine, and with the right tools and mindset, you can conquer stress and pressure and emerge stronger than ever before.

Overcoming Challenges. In this section we delve into the intricate moves between spirituality and creativity, exploring the delicate balance that must be achieved in order to navigate the challenges that arise along the way. Embarking on a creative journey is often accompanied by obstacles, hurdles, and moments of self-doubt. However, by tapping into our spiritual resources, we can find the strength and resilience needed to overcome these challenges. When we engage in any creative endeavor, whether it be writing, painting, or composing music, we open ourselves up to the vulnerability of the creative process. We expose our innermost thoughts and emotions, laying them bare for the world to see. This vulnerability can be daunting, and it is not uncommon to encounter periods of self-doubt and fear. However, it is during these moments that our spirituality can serve as a guiding light, reminding us of our inherent worthiness and the importance of our unique creative expression. One of the primary challenges we face on our creative journey is the fear of failure. The fear that our work will not be well-received, or that it will not live up to our own expectations, can be paralyzing. However, by cultivating a spiritual practice, we can learn to detach ourselves from the outcomes and instead focus on the process itself. Through meditation, prayer, or whatever spiritual practice resonates with us, we can find solace in the present moment, embracing the joy and fulfillment that comes from simply engaging in our creative pursuits. Another challenge we often encounter is the pressure to conform to societal expectations and norms. We may find ourselves questioning whether our creative endeavors are "worthy" or "valuable" based on external standards. However, by deepening our spiritual connection, we can tap into our inner wisdom and intuition, allowing our creative expression to flow authentically from our souls. When we align our creative process with our spiritual truth, we free ourselves from the constraints of societal judgment and open ourselves up to limitless possibilities. Furthermore, as we embark on our creative journey, we may encounter external challenges and obstacles that threaten to derail our progress. These challenges can take many forms, such as financial constraints, time limitations, or lack of support from others. However, by nurturing our spiritual connection, we can tap into a wellspring of inner strength and resilience. Our spirituality becomes a source of inspiration, reminding us of the limitless potential that resides within us. It provides us with the courage to persevere, even in the face of adversity. In conclusion, the balance between spirituality and creativity is not without its challenges. However, by cultivating a deep spiritual connection, we can find the strength and resilience needed to overcome these obstacles. Our spirituality serves as a guiding light, reminding us of our inherent worthiness and the importance of our unique creative expression. By embracing our vulnerability, detaching from outcomes, aligning our creative process with our spiritual truth, and drawing upon our inner strength, we can navigate the challenges on our creative journey and emerge transformed.

CHAPTER SEVEN

Building Effective Habits & Marketing your Creation

We will explore the art of building effective habits.

Habits are the foundation upon which our lives are

built. They shape our actions, determine our

outcomes, and ultimately define who we are as

individuals. If we want to achieve success and make

the most of our time here on earth, it is crucial that

we understand the power of habits and learn how to

cultivate them to our advantage. So, what exactly are

habits? Habits are the automatic behaviors that we

engage in on a daily basis, often without conscious

thought. They are the routines we fall into, the choices

we make without much consideration, and the actions

that have become second nature to us. Habits can be

both positive and negative, and it is up to us to identify and nurture the ones that serve us well. Building effective habits requires intentionality and discipline. It is not enough to simply desire change; we must take deliberate action to make it happen. The first step is to identify the habits that we want to cultivate. What are the behaviors that align with our goals, values, and vision for our lives? Once we have a clear understanding of this, we can begin to design a plan to incorporate these habits into our daily routine. Consistency is key when it comes to building effective habits. It is not enough to practice a behavior once or twice and expect lasting change. We must commit to repeating these actions consistently over time. This may require setting reminders, creating a schedule, or finding an accountability partner who can help keep us on track. By consistently engaging in the desired behavior, we strengthen the neural pathways in our brains, making it easier for us to continue practicing the habit. Another important aspect of building effective habits is to start small. Often, we are tempted to take on too much at once, which can quickly lead to overwhelm and burnout. Instead, we should focus on one habit at a time and break it down into manageable steps. By starting small, we build momentum and increase our chances of success. As the saying goes, "Rome wasn't built in a day," and neither are effective habits. It takes time and patience to create lasting change. Moreover, it is essential to celebrate our progress along the way. Building effective habits is a journey, and every step forward should be acknowledged and celebrated. By recognizing our achievements, we reinforce positive behavior and motivate ourselves to continue moving forward. Whether it is a small milestone or a significant accomplishment, each success brings us closer to our goals. In conclusion, building effective habits is a powerful tool for personal growth and success. By understanding the importance of habits, being intentional in our actions, and staying consistent in our practice, we can transform our lives and reach our full potential. Remember, it's your time to shine, and building effective habits is the key to unlocking your true potential.

Marketing Your Creation In the realm of spirituality and creativity, there exists a delicate balance that needs to be struck. As creators, we are driven by a deep sense of purpose and inspiration, guided by the currents of our soul. Yet, in order to truly share our creations with the world, we must also embrace the art of marketing. Marketing, often seen as a purely commercial endeavor, can sometimes be viewed as antithetical to the spiritual path. However, when approached with the right mindset, marketing can be a powerful tool to amplify the impact of our creations and reach the hearts of those who need them most. At its core, marketing is about connection. It is about forging a bridge between the creator and the audience, enabling a meaningful exchange of ideas, emotions, and experiences. In the context of spirituality and creativity, marketing becomes a means to touch the lives of others, to inspire and uplift, and to create positive change in the world. To effectively market your creation, it is essential to first understand your purpose and intention. What is the underlying message or transformative power that your creation carries? What is the essence of your spirituality and how does it manifest in your creative expression? By delving deep into these questions, you can align your marketing efforts with the authenticity and integrity of your creation. From this place of alignment, it becomes crucial to identify and understand your target audience. Who are the individuals that resonate with your message, that are seeking the very essence of what you have to offer? By gaining insight into their needs, desires, and aspirations, you can craft marketing strategies that speak directly to their hearts, creating a resonance that goes beyond mere transactional exchanges. In the realm of spirituality and creativity, marketing is not about manipulation or coercion. It is about invitation and invitation alone. It is about extending an open hand to those who are ready to receive what you have to offer. By infusing your marketing efforts with the same intention and integrity that guided the creation process, you can create a space of trust and authenticity, where your audience feels seen, heard, and understood. At the heart of successful marketing lies storytelling. Stories have the power to transcend boundaries, to touch the deepest parts of our being, and to awaken the dormant seeds of inspiration within us. By weaving a compelling narrative around your creation, you can captivate the hearts and minds of your audience, drawing them into your world and inviting them to become a part of your journey. In this digital age, technology has become an invaluable ally for creators seeking to market their creations. Websites, social media platforms, and online communities offer boundless opportunities to connect with like-minded individuals, to share your story, and to showcase your creation to a global audience. Embracing these tools while staying true to your spiritual values can amplify the reach and impact of your work, enabling you to touch lives and inspire change on a grand scale.

Ultimately, marketing your creation is not about selling out or compromising your spiritual path. It is about finding the balance between spirituality and creativity, between inner inspiration and outer expression. It is about honoring the sacredness of your creation while also honoring the world that awaits its gifts. By embracing marketing as a means of connection, storytelling, and invitation, you can fulfill your purpose as a creator and share your transformative creations with those who need them most.

CHAPTER EIGHT

Creating a Goal-Oriented Life & Take Time to Reenergize Yourself

We will delve into the process of creating a life that

is centered around goals. By aligning our actions and

aspirations with a clear sense of purpose, we can

unlock our true potential and achieve remarkable

success. It's time to embrace the power of goal-setting

and embark on a journey towards a purposeful and

fulfilling life. Setting meaningful goals is the first step

towards creating a goal-oriented life. The key is to

establish objectives that inspire and motivate us, ones

that resonate deeply with our core values and

aspirations. Take the time to reflect on what truly

matters to you, what drives your passion, and what

brings you a sense of fulfillment. These insights will

serve as the foundation for your goal-setting process. Once you have identified your aspirations, it's important to make them SMART - Specific, Measurable, Achievable, Realistic, and Time-bound. This framework ensures that your goals are well-defined, trackable, and within your reach. By breaking down your broader objectives into smaller, manageable tasks, you will set yourself up for continuous progress and a sense of accomplishment along the way. In addition to setting SMART goals, it's crucial to develop a clear action plan that outlines the steps you need to take to achieve them. This plan will serve as your roadmap and guide you through the journey towards your desired outcomes. Break down your goals into actionable tasks, prioritize them, and create a timeline for their completion. Remember, a goal without a plan is merely a wish - it's your commitment to action that will bring your dreams to life. Alongside setting goals and creating an action plan, it's essential to cultivate a mindset of perseverance and resilience. The path towards achieving our goals is rarely smooth; obstacles and setbacks are inevitable. However, it's in these moments that we have the opportunity to grow, learn, and adapt. Cultivate a positive mindset that embraces challenges as opportunities for growth and views failures as valuable lessons. By staying focused on your goals and maintaining a resilient attitude, you will be better equipped to overcome any hurdles that come your way. Accountability and support are also crucial components of a goal-oriented life. Share your goals with trusted individuals who will hold you accountable and provide encouragement throughout your journey. Remember that you are not alone on this path towards success. Creating a goal-oriented life requires consistent effort and commitment. It's about taking intentional action each day that aligns with your aspirations and propels you towards your goals. Embrace the power of a resilient mindset, you are paving the way for a future filled with purpose and fulfillment.

In the hustle and bustle of our daily lives, it is easy to get caught up in the demands and responsibilities that surround us. Our minds are constantly occupied with work, family, and other obligations, leaving little time for self-care and rejuvenation. However, it is essential to recognize the importance of taking time to re-energize ourselves. In this chapter, we will explore the delicate balance between spirituality and creativity, and how it plays a significant role in our overall well-being. We often overlook the power of these two forces and fail to realize the impact they can have on our lives. Spirituality, in its essence, is about connecting with something greater than ourselves. It is a deeply personal and individual experience that allows us to tap into our inner wisdom and find meaning in the world around us. Whether we practice a specific religion, engage in meditation or mindfulness, or simply spend time in nature, spirituality provides us with a sense of purpose and connection. On the other hand, creativity is the expression of our innermost thoughts, emotions, and ideas. It is the spark that ignites our passion and allows us to bring forth something unique and meaningful into the world. Creativity can manifest in various forms, It is a powerful outlet that enables us to tap into our subconscious mind and unleash our imagination. The interplay between spirituality and creativity is a dynamic one. When we take the time to nurture our spiritual selves, we create a fertile ground for our creative energies to flourish. By connecting with our inner selves and finding peace and tranquility, we open the doors to unlimited inspiration and ideas. In turn, when we engage in creative activities, we nourish our spirituality by expressing our true selves and connecting with the divine source of creativity that resides within us. Taking time to reenergize ourselves is not a luxury; it is a necessity. It is crucial to prioritize self-care and make it a part of our daily routine. By carving out moments of solitude and stillness, we allow ourselves to recharge and replenish our energy reserves. This can be as simple as taking a walk in nature, practicing yoga or meditation, or engaging in a creative hobby that brings us joy and fulfillment. In this fast-paced world, we often neglect the importance of self-care and neglect our spiritual and creative needs. However, by consciously taking the time to re-energize ourselves, we can cultivate a deeper sense of well-being and find balance in our lives. So, let us make a commitment to prioritize our own well-being and embrace the transformative power of spirituality and creativity. It is time to take a step back, reconnect with our inner selves, and allow our spirits to soar.

CHAPTER NINE

Embracing Change and Adapting & Finding More Time To Serve Others

In order to truly shine, there is one crucial skill you must master: Embracing Change and Adapting. Change is an inevitable part of life, and those who are able to embrace it and adapt accordingly are the ones who will thrive. Change can be uncomfortable and unsettling at times. It disrupts our routine, challenges our beliefs, and forces us out of our comfort zone. However, it is during these moments of change that we have the greatest opportunity for growth and success. Change pushes us to explore new possibilities, learn new skills, and discover new strengths within ourselves. To embrace change, we must first shift our mindset. Instead of fearing change, we need to view it as an opportunity for growth and self-improvement. Change is not something to be avoided or resisted, but rather something to be embraced and welcomed. It is through change that we can break free from the limitations of our old ways and step into a brighter, more fulfilling future. Adapting to change requires flexibility and resilience. We must be willing to let go of old habits and beliefs that no longer serve us. It may be uncomfortable at first, but as we let go of the old, we make space for the new. We must be open to new ideas, new perspectives, and new approaches. This willingness to adapt allows us to navigate through the ever-changing landscape of life with grace and ease. Embracing change and adapting also requires a willingness to take risks. Change often involves stepping into the unknown and venturing outside of our comfort zone. But it is in these moments of uncertainty and discomfort that we have the greatest opportunity for growth. We must be willing to take calculated risks, try new things, and push ourselves beyond our perceived limits. Only then can we truly embrace change and adapt to whatever comes our way. It's important to remember that change is not a one-time event, but a constant presence in our lives. The world is constantly evolving, and so must we. By embracing change and adapting, we not only survive but thrive in this ever-changing world. We become more resilient, more resourceful, and more capable of facing any challenge that comes our way. So, my dear reader, I encourage you to embrace change and adapt. It's your time to shine, and by mastering this crucial skill, you will be unstoppable. Embrace the unknown, step outside of your comfort zone, and be willing to take risks. Embrace change as an opportunity for growth and self-improvement. Embrace change as the catalyst for your success. Embrace change and watch yourself shine brighter than ever before.

In the realm of spirituality and creativity, there exists a delicate balance that can be found in the act of serving others. When we embark on a journey of self-discovery and self-expression, it is important to remember that our gifts and talents are not meant solely for our own benefit. We have the power to uplift, inspire, and make a positive impact on those around us. Finding ways to serve others through our spirituality and creativity can be a deeply fulfilling and transformative experience. It allows us to connect with the essence of our being and tap into a higher purpose. As we navigate this path, we may discover that there are endless possibilities to fine more ways to serve others. One way to serve others is to use our creative talents to spread messages of love, hope, and compassion. Whether it be through writing, painting, music, or any other form of artistic expression, we have the ability to touch the hearts and souls of those who encounter our work. By infusing our creations with intention and a desire to uplift others, we can inspire change and make a difference in the world. Additionally, serving others through spirituality means recognizing the interconnectedness of all beings. When we deepen our spiritual practice, we begin to understand that we are not separate from the world around us. This awareness opens our hearts and minds to the needs and struggles of others. We can offer support, kindness, and empathy to those who are in need, knowing that our actions have the power to bring comfort and healing. Furthermore, serving others can manifest in the form of volunteering or engaging in community service. By actively participating in initiatives that aim to improve the lives of others, we contribute to the greater good. This can be through lending a helping hand to those less fortunate, participating in environmental conservation efforts, or supporting causes that align with our values. Through these acts of service, we find fulfillment and purpose in knowing that we are making a positive impact on the lives of others. Ultimately, finding more ways to serve others is not only a testament to our own growth and selflessness, but it is also a reflection of the divine energy that flows through us. When we align our spirituality and creativity with the intention of serving others, we tap into a source of inspiration and guidance that transcends our individual selves. In doing so, we become channels for love, compassion, and healing in the world. So, as you continue to explore the balance between spirituality and creativity, remember to seek out opportunities to serve others. Allow your passions and gifts to be a conduit for positive change. Embrace the power you possess to uplift and inspire. For in the act of serving others, you will find a profound sense of purpose and fulfillment that transcends the boundaries of the self.

CHAPTER TEN

Living with Passion and Purpose

Living with Passion and Purpose In this chapter, we will delve into the incredible power of living with passion and purpose. It is a journey that each one of us must embark upon, for it is in this journey that we truly come alive and discover the depths of our potential. Passion is the fuel that ignites our souls and propels us forward. It is the fire within us that burns brightly, driving us to pursue our dreams and desires with unwavering enthusiasm. When we live with passion, we tap into a boundless energy that fuels our every action, infusing our lives with a sense of vibrancy and zest. But passion alone is not enough; it must be coupled with purpose. Purpose is the compass that guides us, giving our passion direction and meaning. It is the why behind everything we do, the reason that fuels the fire within us. When we live with purpose, our actions become intentional and aligned with our values. We become driven by a higher calling, a sense of mission that transcends the mundane and propels us towards greatness. Living with passion and purpose requires us to tap into our true selves and discover what truly makes us come alive. It is about uncovering our unique talents and gifts, and using them to make a positive impact in the world. It is about embracing our passions and pursuing them wholeheartedly, regardless of the challenges and obstacles that may come our way. To live with passion and purpose, we must first cultivate self-awareness. We must take the time to reflect on what truly makes us happy and fulfilled. What brings us joy? What activities make us lose track of time? What values do we hold dear? By asking ourselves these questions, we can gain insight into our passions and align them with our purpose. Once we have gained clarity on our passions and purpose, the next step is to take action. We must be willing to step out of our comfort zones and pursue our dreams with unbridled enthusiasm. It may require us to face our fears, overcome obstacles, and push through self-doubt. But it is in these moments of discomfort and uncertainty that we truly grow and thrive. Living with passion and purpose also requires us to cultivate a mindset of gratitude and resilience. We must be grateful for the opportunities and blessings that come

our way, even in the face of adversity. We must learn

from our failures and setbacks, using them as stepping

stones towards our ultimate success. With a resilient

mindset, we can persevere in the face of challenges

and continue to move forward, undeterred by the

obstacles that may arise. When we live with passion

and purpose, we not only transform our own lives,

but we also inspire and uplift those around us. Our

enthusiasm becomes contagious, spreading like

wildfire and igniting the spark within others. We

become beacons of light, showing others what is

possible when we live in alignment with our passions

and purpose. So, my dear reader, I urge you to

embrace the power of living with passion and

purpose. Discover what truly makes your heart sing and pursue it with unwavering determination. Align your actions with your values and let your light shine brightly for all to see. For in living with passion and purpose, you will discover the true essence of your being and unlock the limitless potential within you.

NOW, GO AND SHINE!

Learn More About: Sura Khan

www.surakhan.net

www.thechambersseries.com

Instagram: @vse1surakhan

Twitter: @Surakhan11

Checkout the TV Series —Written & Directed by SURA KHAN Now streaming on TUBI, PRIME VIDEO, FAWESOM & REVEEL TV

E-Mail: Info@surakhan.net

Made in the USA
Middletown, DE
30 October 2023

41528552R00066